TRIUMPH HOUSE
Poetry with a Purpose

CHRISTIAN CELEBRATIONS FROM SCOTLAND, IRELAND & WALES 2000

Edited by

Kelly Deacon

First published in Great Britain in 2000 by
TRIUMPH HOUSE
Remus House,
Coltsfoot Drive,
Woodston,
Peterborough, PE2 9JX
Telephone (01733) 898102

HB ISBN 1 86161 693 7
SB ISBN 1 86161 698 8

FOREWORD

Each year Triumph House launches its regional series of poems - bringing forth to the reader a mixed blend of Christian opinions and expressions on today's modern issues. Prayers, messages of faith and Christian perspectives on life are all shared and defined withing these pages, helping the intimate bond between reader and author to be discovered. The poems may vary in both style and theme but each is a unique insight and inspiration, brought to you from the power of the working mind.

This collection has been compiled from the areas of Scotland, Ireland and Wales, and celebrates the heartaches and the joys of modern Christian verse. In true poetic style this book is sure to both encourage and delight for many years to come.

Kelly Deacon
Editor

CONTENTS

THE BAND OF HOPE

Damply defiant in the drizzle,
Like General Custer's men,
Only introverted.
Brassily blowing
At each other
Until it's time
For a breath,
And to pass the cap
Around the only three
Gathered together
In His name.

David Madeira-Cole
Wales

I REITERATE

I have seen the face of God
In the smile of a babe.
I have heard the voice of God
In the cuckoo's call.
I have inhaled the perfume of God
From a hedgerow honeysuckle.
I have savoured the taste of God
In a morsel of home-made bread.
I have felt the presence of God
In mosque, synagogue, temple and church
And in all the places
Sacred to the daughters and sons
Of women and men.

Now, sophisticated friends and others
Burdened and weary with too much knowledge
Will cynically say:
So what's new about these observations?
Such truisms are as ancient as the hills.
With old age coming on you're turning
To the trite.

They are, quite probably, right.
But one cannot have too much
Of a good thing.
Certain statements require
Constant repetition.
And, besides, God's truth can take
The battering of reiteration.

Reginald Massey
Wales

SILENT SERVICE

Darkness, lit by flickering candles.
Cold air warmed by fellowship.
Silent prayer, quiet thoughts to God.
Images of rocky heights and ever changing seas
Baring a constant witness to God's majesty.
A silent chain with all those people
Who have sat, as we are sitting now.
In silent prayerful meditation, a communion with God.
Since ancient days your people Lord have worshipped.
Within these safe grey stone walls.
An everlasting faithful prayerful witness,
To the unending glory of our God.

G A Ayling
Wales

THE POTTER

We are but clay upon the wheel of life,
The Master Potter forms as he sees best.
He forms and trims with wire, hand and knife,
And having formed, he puts us to the test.

But some are less than perfect in the mould,
And some are by the fires of life, distort.
Those very fires to some bring streaks of gold,
While others, flawed, from their design fall short.

The fiery trials of life give some a sheen,
An added lustre to the potter's art.
But some are crazed, and some are never seen,
Their defects place them in a world apart.

But all are touched by his strong, tender hands,
And all are loved, imperfect though they be.
Their faults are known, but yet he understands,
He by his sacrifice has set us free.

So though imperfect, yet we still may serve,
And to our Master prove a thing of worth.
If from His will for us, we do not swerve,
But seek the purposes that gave us birth.

W McIntyre
Scotland

WHAT REALLY MATTERS?

The end period before the Reformation
saw the Christian religion become man-centred.
The reformers brought back
the Christian religion which is God-centred.

This reforming is an ongoing process
with all striving to gain heaven's access.
I'm Baptist. I'm Pentecostal. I'm Brethren.
I'm Methodist. I'm C of E. I'm C of S. I'm confused?

Yet all these interpretations
are recorded in the New Testament information.
To be dogmatic that our view is right
may suggest that other views are wrong.
Seek ye first God's light,
for He seeks the born again throng.

'Ye must be born again,'
said Jesus to a professor of theology.
Nicodemus was his name -
even he was confused by Jesus' claim.

Confused still? Then consider this:
A man had a variety of ducks,
each species in their own pens.
Each had their own style.
Along comes the flood
raising the ducks above their pens;
to be as one - together,
as in heaven above.

Christians of various denominations,
when flooded with the Holy Spirit
can express their source of unity
without the need for uniformity.

J Henderson Lightbody
Scotland

HE WILL BE WITH YOU

He will be with you in your hour of need,
wherever you go *He* will precede,
knowing that *He* will be waiting there for you,
surely your faith will forever grow.

> *He* will be with you whenever you call
> accepting your failings whatever befalls,
> *He* will be there awaiting your call,
> yes *He* will be there awaiting your call.

Whenever the sun shines bright in the sky,
and the winds blow the clouds as they roll by,
even when the heavy rain does fall,
a beautiful rainbow across the sky *He* will sprawl.

> *He* will be with you whenever you call
> accepting your failings whatever befalls,
> *He* will be there awaiting your call,
> yes *He* will be there awaiting your call.

He will be there if you will only believe,
giving you strength to soothe your grief,
restoring your faith should you go astray,
guiding you on a path to a better way.

> *He* will be with you whenever you call
> accepting your failings whatever befalls,
> *He* will be there awaiting your call,
> yes *He* will be there awaiting your call.

Robert Gerald
Wales

HOW I FEEL!

I look forward to a day,
When there's more time to pray,
More time to love and care,
More time to read and share.

Twenty-four little hours make my day,
And sometimes I find it hard to say,
The things God puts on my heart,
But I know I should play my part.

I ask myself sometimes why does God need me?
He told me he chose me and my heart just filled with glee,
I don't understand and probably never will,
But this one thing I know, he loves me still.

Lyndsey McDougall
Ireland

Morning Beauteous

A morning bright and brand new,
geraniums ablaze in the window;
roses, lavender, stocks and honeysuckle
                    scent the air:
God! What a morning, I declare.

A morning of happy smiling faces,
cheery greetings, exchanged;
hearts of troubled souls, lightened
                    everywhere:
God! What a morning, I declare.

A morning for a riverside walk,
be at peace, with oneself, and the world;
birds sing gaily, trout rise for fare,
God! What a morning I declare.

A morning to travel, far,
countryside and town, look new;
sun-drenched park and bands a'playing
                    there:
God! What a morning, I declare.

A morning to paint the fence,
tend the crops, spray the roses;
laze on a bench, reading poems, rare:
God! What a morning, I declare.

A morning to go to church,
to thank God, for his many blessings;
help a friend who may be in need of a prayer:
God! What a morning, I declare.

A morning to put your house in order,
open your eyes, and your heart;
for the dawn to come, prepare:
God! What a morning, I declare.

Bernard
Wales

PARABLES

A poor old widow's story,
Dear Lord, you once did tell,
Who gave her last coin freely,
Not caring what befell.
Teach us today, Our Father,
To give so selflessly
To help the weak and starving,
And ease their poverty.

A wayward son, you told us,
Who had great wealth to burn,
When he had spent his fortune
He knew not where to turn.
Teach us today, Our Father,
No matter where we roam,
The path which you have shown us
Will always lead us home.

You taught us of a sower
Who went to scatter seeds,
And how the shoots were stifled
And strangled by the weeds.
Today, let our hearts, Father,
Be fertile soil for you,
So that your words can blossom
And flower within us too.

Helen Royle Edwards
Wales

NATURE'S CHORAL UNION

There is music in the mountains that no human can contest -
it's a strange and heavenly chorale and the songs are Nature's best!
Such tiny creatures singing with a love we cannot comprehend,
in praise of their Creator, their Master and their Friend!
A lark sings in sweet ecstasy as he penetrates the sky
and a blackbird trills in harmony as he gaily passes by!
There's a pretty little bluebird twittering in its cosy nest
and a brightly coloured pheasant tries to chortle his very best.
The majestic golden eagle shrieks loudly as he swoops to catch
his prey -
whilst the shrill call of a seagull echoes wildly across Spey Bay!
A balmy breeze caresses heather bells that nod in silent prayer
and the rare sight of an osprey appears to show that he is there!
It's a halleluia chorus from God's creatures great and small
in praise of His wondrous love and grace as 'He conducts' life
for us all!

Mary E A Poynton
Scotland

I'M SIMPLY JUST A GUEST OF GOD

Whenever I'm alone with you,
My mind has got the time
To find a very special peace
Of a very special kind,
Because I'm in the silence
Of a very special place,
And no one here around me
Seems to know my face.

I'm simply just a guest of God:
Wherever God may choose,
He'll walk me to most any place
Where my thoughts and cares I'll lose.
He'll listen to my silent prayer
Amidst all man-made noise,
And in the depths of silence
I'm sure I hear His voice:

Oh come to Me, all weary folk,
And leave your cares behind.
For I will offer Peace and Love
Of a very special kind.
- Not the kind that man has made,
Or his promise to fulfil.
So come to Me in prayer and thought,
Abandon all you will.

Your load is much too heavy,
Your day it's busy too:
But come to Me and stay a while
For I'll take care of you.
'Oh pray to Me' that's all I ask,
And surely don't ask more.
And I will keep you safe by Me
Till you reach Heaven's shore.

And talk to Me most any day
Whenever you may choose:
Bring your troubles to My door
And anxious woes defuse.
I hope now in your silence
I've left you feeling strong.
Enjoy the life you have on Earth,
One day it shall be gone.

Kathleen Y Ambler
Scotland

NORTH OF IRELAND CHRISTIANITY

I see a structure in society where people gather to
worship Nimrod within the nation's capital . . . it
speaks a flesh-tone language, and is working in the
social scene.

'All animals are equal, but some animals are more equal -
than others;' it's a sad reality - North of Ireland -
Christianity.
There's a melting clock on every wall - its chime:
'Let the night begin, for tomorrow we die.'
Welcome to your millennium . . .

You people on the streets
You people at death's door
You people who remain nameless
You people who rule the nation with guns
You people clothed in stars
You people who work for a livin'
You people who numb reality
You people who reach for a cup of coffee . . . yes -
friends, that is you and I, clinically moulded while
our brother is shot down in front of a vast audience.
Then again, you can always switch channels, or turn
the television off!

It's been one thousand, nine hundred and seventy years
since you left friend, I just thought I had to say that.
Brothers, sisters, around the world, the master is
near, and while I ponder on heaven . . . smoking a
cigarette - well, none of us is perfect.

J Sutton
Ireland

THE ANCIENT OF DAYS

Our Lord is described as the 'Ancient of days',
So ageless, unchanging, in all of His ways,
No furrows of stress, disfigure that face,
But beauty of youth, and immeasurable grace.

Though while He is God, yet showed He humility,
For the promised Messiah, became a reality;
Displaying to all, by His actions supreme,
The Biblical promise, was not just a dream.

The glory of God, fully resided in Him,
Yet through many trials, it never grew dim,
Though veiled in His flesh, it ever shone through,
In miraculous acts, and great teaching too.

This wonderful Lord, who became a mere man,
To deal with our sin, through Salvation's plan,
Involved such an act of amazing grace,
We are bound to worship before His face.

To worship Him who paid our debt,
As demands of 'The Law' were fully met,
On the cross of shame that Easter day,
By the Saviour of men, such a fearful way.

As we've thought of Him, so wondrous fair,
Words fail to come, He's beyond compare,
How can mere man describe this one,
'The ancient of days', God's beloved Son.

Though at least it is obvious, we've had a try,
That He fills our vision, we cannot deny,
For the time is coming, when we'll see His face

'Glory to God, we are saved by grace'.

John G Studley
Wales

TO GIVE A CHILD

To give a child a present,
To see a smiling face,
And if it makes you smile,
In your heart you've made a space
To give, and not to moan,
Will make God very happy,
As He sits upon His throne.
So please be kind to all children
Even if they're not your own,
And to give at Christmas time,
God watches from His throne.

Isobel Buchanan
Scotland

REVIVAL

Wouldn't it be wonderful if we could see
In the millennium a mass revival of Christianity
People rejoicing, the bells would be ringing
Everyone happy, hymns of praise they'd be singing

All nations true Christians this my plea
Then what a joyous world it would be
All denominations merge into one
In the millennium pray God's will be done

In the year two thousand, no more hate or wars
God's love for everyone will open all doors
Christianity must come back to stay
This is my prayer at each close of the day

We don't need riches, fortune, or fame
When we can be blessed by God's holy name
What good are treasures, what are they worth
Compared with God's promise, the meek shall inherit the earth.

E Dowler
Wales

INTO A NEW ERA

Into a new era
The old tonight bids us goodbye
Another step into our future
God has given us another new century to try
To try again for the victory
In our homes, our work, our towns
To show to others in our world
That God is still hanging around.
Into a new era
The good shall conquer the bad
Now is the time for rejoicing
The new era has no time for being sad
For being sad over what we should have done
Or what we could have said
God in this new era now upon us
Has better things lying in store up ahead
So in this new era
Lean and put your trust in him
Let his hand guide the way
For your soul within.

Deborah Strain
Ireland

Choose You This Day

You have heard the gospel message, and accept it is true,
And fully understand exactly what you must do -
Coming in faith to Jesus, acknowledging all your sin,
As you open your heart's door, and ask the Saviour in.

But does another voice say that there is no hurry -
'You have plenty of time, so why at present then worry?'
But this subtle suggestion, which makes you hesitate,
May mean you'll postpone this decision, till sadly 'tis too late.

For the scriptural command is seek the Lord while you may,
As, like a vapour, each life is passing swiftly away,
With there being for none any complete guarantee
That the dawn of tomorrow they will definitely see.

So won't you seize this opportunity while yet you still can?
For God's Holy Spirit shall not always strive with man,
And He plainly declares the accepted time is now
To come to the Saviour, and at His feet humbly bow.

Why not follow the example of Joshua of old,
Who, the assembled tribes of Israel solemnly told -
This day choose to whom you will service afford,
But as for me and my house, we will serve the Lord.

Yes, choose you this day the master you'll follow,
For your eternal destiny is sealed here below
By the decision you take to either reject or embrace
The One who abundantly can save through His infinite grace.

How long will you then between two opinions halt?
For, if you miss God's salvation, 'twill be but your own fault;
So delay no longer, I urge you, but make Christ now your choice,
That the very angels in heaven may have great cause to rejoice.

Ian Caughey
Ireland

JESUS I NEED YOU

Jesus I need you
To lighten my days
So help me my Saviour
To cherish your ways
I need you I need you
Throughout all my life
Oh help me dear Jesus
To cope with life's strife

Jesus I need you
Look down from above
Enfold me and fill me
With thy sacred love
I need you I need you
By thought word and deed
I pray to you daily
To answer my need

Mary Hudson
Scotland

A THIEF IN THE NIGHT

The Lord will return unexpectedly
As a thief comes in the night
To take those who belong to him
To realms of eternal light
He will call his chosen and faithful ones
Out of this sinful earth
To claim their true inheritance
They were promised with new birth.

They have waited long
For his return
Their names are written down
In the book of life
Before the world began
And all to God are known
I ask a question
As you sit and read
This poem in your chair
If the Lord would suddenly
                    return tonight
Is your name written there.

Christine Williams
Wales

INCH ABBEY

In the walls of the ruined abbey
The rooks have made their home.
If you stand there in the silence
You feel you are not alone.
You can hear the pad of sandalled feet,
The chanting of a prayer.
The monks who once dwelt in this place
Their spirits are still there.

Across the green now tangled field
Lies the lake where they used to fish,
And here is the bakestone still intact
Where they cooked their simple dish.
Part of the dining hall remains,
A few cracked and broken slates
Where once they ate their humble meal
From simple wooden plates.

Just sit awhile in the silence
Hark! 'tis the evening prayer.
The ghosts of the monks are passing,
The rooks just sit and stare.
I wonder can they see them pass,
The monks who once dwelt there.

Isobel Laffin
Ireland

THE WELSH CHAPEL

Welsh Chapel, granite hard and unadorned,
Thrusting its way into the world,
As if to say, 'Challenge me if you dare!'
Built by our fathers in a world that had no measure
    of weakness.
While, from the open windows, the sound of singing
    pours;
Lyrical tenor and soprano, wondrous full contralto and
    deep, moving bass.
All so naturally blending together, rising and falling;
A volume of sound that stops the heart and fills the mind.
As though, for those few moments, the world is forgotten
    and ceased to be
The hard taskmaster that we know so well.

H Cullen
Wales

GIFTS AND TALENTS

Trials and temptation I already have
Fears and doubts I have them too
But I must learn to trust my Saviour
Because he will simply carry me through

Gifts and talents we have many
But they're not really good enough
If we don't use them to tell others
Of a father and his love.

So let us stand and work together
From this world we've been set free
Let's not fight or cause division
Simply hope and trust in thee.

Let's spend time with our creator
Prayer and reading day by day
For he has a plan to lead and guide us
And he'll open our eyes and show the way.

Kenneth Ferguson
Scotland

THE HIGHER HAND

Spinning with arms outstretched,
Farther than ever before.
Fingertips reaching, tingling
Closer to the cool night sky.

To a midnight blue backcloth,
Twinkling with mysterious stars.
Until suddenly; I'm thinking;
Space and clearer vision.

All that is ill departs,
Vanishes in the shrinking.
Whilst the best illuminates;
Filling, crowding, and swelling.

What precious, timely, movement
This dwarfing and expansion,
Eliminating wrath and pain,
Concentrating hope and pleasure.

I come inside at last,
Softly shut the door.
When gentle morning comes
I shall start all over.

Morag Wright
Scotland

DAWN OF A THOUSAND YEARS

Be at peace with the midnight sky,
And look on the beauty of the stars,
Jewels in the black velvet backdrop of forever.
The moon journeys across the heavens,
Awaiting the rise of a greater light.
Come, arise, from a dream within a dream,
And let your heart beat with anticipation and hope.
As the curtain of night fades into the morning light,
Stars lose their luminosity and the moon surrenders,
Yielding her beauty to the unfolding dawn.
Come, be caught up in the rapture of this moment.
Abandon all sorrows, fears, and past regrets.
Greet the sun arising from behind the purple mountains.
The sky becomes a mosaic of brilliant colours,
And the soul rejoices in the beauty of this day,
Giving thanks to God for this new age of the Spirit.
An age of hope, reconciliation and Love.

Wilma Hogg
Scotland

A PRISONER WENT FREE

They led forth the Master
To be nailed to a tree;
While from a dark cell,
A prisoner went free.

He didn't deserve it,
It was only by grace;
For this pure Lamb of God
Had taken his place.

I too sat alone
In the dungeon of sin,
I was hopeless and helpless
God's favour to win.

But this blessed Saviour
Died on the tree;
Yes, He took my place,
So that I could go free.

Now I'm a love-slave,
A debtor to grace;
Jesus captured my heart,
The One Who died in my place.

O prisoner in the dungeon,
There is hope for you too;
The Saviour has died
And rose again for you.

Though condemned already,
On the Saviour believe;
His Blood atoned for your sin,
Now His pardon receive.

Joy Patterson
Ireland

A PRAYER TO DIVINITY

I thought
      I'd found you,
I thought
      I'd lost you.

How can I be so vain!
How can I be so mean!
Claiming the credit,
thinking I do it all.
Instead of understanding
you are, have been, and will always be there,
no matter what,
for whoever in need,
be it them, she,
he, us, me.

The credits are yours, thank thee!
But they make you a man-made god, 'He, the Lord'
. . . and again I feel lost . . . again I have no vote . . .
I am sure that is not really so. I am sure you are for us all.
Dear Divinity take care of me!

RubiSquirrell
Scotland

LIFE WITH NO REGRETS

Four score years have passed in life,
Was once sweetheart, mother and wife.

My man was faithful, true and strong,
Fifty years together, he never did me wrong.

Worked together to make things go right,
Even when tired, battled through the night.

We got through life, accepted our fate,
No blame to others, no malice or hate.

Together we travelled, viewed many places
Respected friends, remembered many faces.

Now I'm alone from day to day
I have great faith, I live my way.

Twilight years may have descended,
Good memories are my treasures
To be remembered.

Glad Davies
Wales

ATROCITY

Lord, so much is going on that we don't understand.
Hurricanes and earthquakes, causing death throughout the land.
Wars and bad disruptions on every continent
Everywhere, the people are feeling discontent.
We pray that you will help us, to get it all to cease.
Bring love and understanding, so that there will be peace
Quieten the earth, to settle and be still.
Make us all your children, if that is your will.

Margaret Rankin
Scotland

LITTLE GIRL IN A PHOTOGRAPH

A little girl stands
in a vast green place.
Calm, casual, cool, uncomplicated,
Frozen in time and space.

What are her thoughts, her questions,
why is she there?
Her parents, her guardians,
Are they anywhere near?

Is she abandoned, is she playing,
Pushed out from the crowd?
Is she laughing or posing,
perhaps crying out loud?

Who is she, why is she,
what does she mean?
The unknown child,
on the carpet of green.

Is she anybody's child,
Is she everybody's child?
Is she a child of the world,
Is she just . . . a child?

Is any child . . . just a child,
Or, is it the child of us all.
Does it matter, who the parents,
Is the child not the parent of all?

J Doyle
Scotland

ABBA FATHER

Abba Father you made me
In your holy way.
For you are the potter
I am but the clay.

You shaped me for your good
I don't have a say.
For you are the potter
I am but the clay.

Though sometimes I fall
I will not break away
For you are the potter
I am but the clay.

In the heat I will harden
I will stand though I sway.
For you are the potter
I am but the clay.

You know Abba Father
You made me this way.
For you are the potter
I am but the clay.

Elizabeth Hughes
Wales

UNTITLED

From mighty mammoths, elephants and whales,
To the miniature perfection of a baby's fingernails.
From planets whirling far beyond the sky,
To grains of sand on sea's periphery.

So many wonders spread the earth abroad
How can man doubt the presence of a God?

So let us give our praise and thanks to Him
Whose generosity our needs supplies,
And pray that He will save us from ourselves
Nor let us spoil His earthly paradise.

M S Marshall
Scotland

2000 AD

Welcome the new millennium
　　　In country and in town;
May the year 2000AD
　　　In history go down.

Let flags on public buildings fly
　　　And all the church bells peal,
And every person in the land
　　　Strive for the common weal.

Let all who dwell within these shores
　　　Rejoice in park and street
Adorned with flowers and bunting
　　　An era new to greet.

Fireworks, music and pageantry
　　　Proclaim the year has come,
And Britons now can celebrate
　　　The new millennium.

Glynfab John
Wales

OUR CHURCH

Nestled in the corner,
    so steadfast, strong and sure,
There stands for me another Home
    wherein such peace exists.
Each Sabbath as I sit and pray,
    my thankfulness I give.
My blessings here are many,
    new friendships firm and true.
My days have far more meaning
    now I *see* as I do look,
and when I leave this Home grown dear
    until another day,
A handshake seals what I have learned,
    in this quiet House of Peace.

Janet Parkes
Scotland

EASTER RESPONSES

The murderer said, 'He took my sin
I should be there instead of Him
The man called Jesus took my place
Amazing Love
Amazing Grace'

The rich man said, 'I'll find the room
to place the Lord in my own tomb
For when he cried
Dear Lord, forgive
I know He died that I might live'

The woman said, 'He is not there
The grave is empty, the tomb is bare,
He spoke to me in a gentle voice
Weep not, my child
Believe, rejoice'

The doubter said, 'I won't believe
unless assurance I receive
If I can but touch the nail-scarred hands
then I'll believe
and understand'
'Forgive me Lord, I cry to you
for all that I have put you through
For failing Lord, to watch and pray
Forgive me Lord
This Easter Day'

C MacIntyre
Scotland

CHILDREN

Children running round about,
Children free as air;
Children happy, children glad,
Children dark and fair;
God gave us a little child,
To live with us on earth;
Showing us His loving care,
By dear Lord Jesus' birth;
By His life He showed us all
What we ought to be;
By His death He saved us all
On dark Calvary;
Listen to His words of love,
Come you unto Me;
You will have eternal life,
And from sin be free.

Isabella Buchan
Scotland

WHEN I HEAR YOUR TRUMPET CALL

Lord; I hear you calling,
I hear you as I pray.
Lord; ring out your trumpet;
show to me the way.

For I know that I'm a sinner
and my soul is falling fast.
Lord; like the walls of Jericho,
I tremble at your blast.

So ring out your trumpet loudly,
for my soul is Devil bound,
and I will walk with you so proudly
when I hear that trumpet sound.

It tumbles down my ignorance;
it dries confusion's tears,
and I am filled with glory
for my future holds no fears.

Yes, I will walk beside you,
I will face the Devil's gall,
and my soul it will come running,
when I hear your trumpet call.

So ring out that trumpet loudly,
and show to me the way,
for my heart it beats so proudly
when upon my knees I pray.

I pray to God in Heaven;
the keeper of my soul.
For in His mighty army,
I will this day enrol.

So let it echo through the forests
and down the valleys ring.
For I am bathed in glory
when I hear your trumpet sing.

Bryon J Jones
Wales

THE INVITATION

I came to see you today, Lord
I knocked on the door of Your heart
You opened it wide
And said: 'Come on inside
Come sit with Me
And we'll talk'

Please come and see me today, Lord
Please knock at the door of my heart
I'll open it wide
And say: 'Come on inside
Come sit with me
And we'll talk'

Thelma Roberts
Wales

THE GREAT JUBILEE

'Just another Hogmanay' they said, 'why all the fuss?'
Is that really all it is?
A new century,
A new millennium.
Two thousand years ago the Son of God was born
And walked this earth, and died and rose again.
So now they want to have a party -
The biggest ever!
Just another Hogmanay;
Another excuse to get drunk.
But - a new century,
A new millennium,
Something to celebrate -
'Whose birthday did you say it is?
Jesus! What's God got to do with it?'
A new century,
A new millennium,
Two thousand years;
Why can't they understand that He still lives
So we have cause to celebrate?
His life and death and rising changed the world
Two thousand years ago.
A new century,
A new millennium,
And Jesus lives
Within the hearts of all who own His name.
So celebrate with us the year Two Thousand,
Christ's Jubilee;
For without Him there is no new millennium,
But just another Hogmanay.

S Clement
Scotland

THE MILLENNIAL PRINCE OF PEACE

Two thousand years have passed since Jesus came
Into earth's time from heaven's eternity:
Came to bring Peace to birth, and to proclaim
Death upon war and man's perversity,
To bring His rest to lands beset by Rome,
To cleanse all sin from 'Salem's Temple Dome'.

Two thousand years have passed since Jesus came
To live in love and loveliness 'mongst men,
To die upon that Cross of saving shame
Then rise in power to endless life. What then?
He entered heaven The Prince of Life and Peace
To reign in righteousness without surcease.

Two thousand years have passed since Jesus came,
Now come to our own times, He says always
In gentlest whisper, 'Peace, ever the same,
Be unto you, and joy throughout your days.'
Of Time Divine let's ask a question due:
'Why welcome one millennium, not two?'

These twenty centuries their time have run,
Yet heaven's sweet Dove of Peace alights below
On our sad warring world by strife undone,
On troubled East and stricken Kosovo.
Oh that our hearts might ever open be
To take the Peace He gives so willingly!

Two thousand years have passed since Jesus came.
His perfect Peace abides in fullest prime.
Man builds his Greenwich Dome, his 'Pleasure Dome', a name
To worship wealth, pomp, power, and formal time.
We fear when all is said and done, that then,
The Dome is not for Jesus, but for men.

John Gillespie
Scotland

WHOLLY SATURDAY
(Reflections of friend's reaction to my divorce)

Look what they have done
To your hand Mum
Look what they have done
Your hand is naked, ashamed

All the rings it once flashed
Look what they have done to your hand
Take another walk out, Mum
Look what they have done

Search out a way forward Mum
Look what they have done
To your hand, taken off the symbols
Look what they have done to your hand.

S M Thompson
Ireland

DAILY A REALITY

Make communion, Lord, with Thee
daily a reality;
Please, guard my relationship
with You in heaven's fellowship.
Be my Helper every day
as, in need, to You I pray;
Grant Your Spirit's strength, in me,
To accept Truth's ministry.

Wonder of my life, this joy,
joy in You, none can destroy.
Help me give the time I owe
to You and the folks I know.
Help me not the Spirit grieve
when I doubt and disbelieve;
May I look to You for power,
serve you fruitfully each hour.

For Your counsel, Lord, I plead
as for me You intercede;
May my spirit docile be,
loving You, as You love me.
By Your hand, and gracious grip,
lead me in heaven's fellowship;
Make communion, Lord, with Thee
daily a reality.

Ken Millar
Scotland

A PRAYER

A closet with a fast-barred door
Gain's entrance to the 'House of Store',
Ask, seek and knock, with answers each,
Let's humbly bow, the throne to reach.

There's not a word, which we can say,
Already known before we pray.
Yet God desires to be enquired of,
We cannot ever pray enough.

To supplicate, what wondrous privilege,
To intercede with humble verbiage.
In giving thanks for answered prayer,
Encouraged every burden share.

God knows alone just what is best,
E'en though we pray with utmost zest.
There is a chance, we pray amiss,
Arrange things first, then seek His bliss.

The more we pray, the more we plead,
Gives indication of felt need.
What weak and helpless souls we are,
Yet strength and power comes from afar.

James Neilly
Scotland

JESUS IS YOUR SAVIOUR

May the Good Lord bless and keep you
Each and every day,
All the things your heart desires
The Lord will bring your way.

A little prayer each morning
Will help you through the day,
Simply say 'I love you Lord,
Please guide me on my way.'

Praise His love with glory,
Magnify His name,
And when you meet on Judgement Day,
I know He'll call your name.

Jamesie Gardner
Scotland

CHRISTMAS IS BUT ONCE A YEAR

When December comes, we start to fear,
There's gifts to wrap and cards to write,
So much to do before the night!
We push and we shove, and wear ourselves out,
Is this what Christmas is all about?
Our birthdays come around, we receive
Gifts and cards, if our family forgot us,
We'd consider them hard, but along comes
Christmas, our Saviour's birthday, and we
Shrug Him off in such a casual way.
We're carried along with the glitter and glimmer,
Of a world without Christ, where their future
Is dimmer,
So help us Dear Lord, as the world has a
Mirthday, to celebrate Christmas, as our Saviour's
Birthday,
To greet the great day with calm and delight,
As we recognise our Saviour's might.
His gift to us is the gift of love,
What more could we ask of our Saviour above?
But He promises peace, and everlasting joy too,
Paid for by Him, especially for you.

Gwen Pemberton
Wales

A HOLY MILESTONE YEAR

Regarding this new millennium
People question; 'What is to happen . . .
2000 years since the Saviour's birth,
Will it herald His 2nd Advent?'

If we believe that Christ was born
To rule, one day, in glory -
The time and venue, God will set,
By His own divine authority.

So, let's commit this ancient planet,
Its mystery and its glory, to Him
Who'll separate darnel from the wheat
And make perfection of it.

Before 'Omega time' we must make sure,
Be well prepared - our faith secure.
Free, of ill dreams that destroy . . .
Wait, in faith, His Holy Advent Time.

Past, present, future - together,
Because of the 'King of Glory'.

Marion de Bruyn
Wales

LOST

Where are you Lord?
Have I gone deaf?
I turn to the left,
And am bereft.

Where are you Lord?
I look to see,
I turn to the right,
Have I lost my sight?

Where are you Lord?
On this path of life,
You said you would,
Help me in my strife!

There's no going back,
Of that I'm sure,
I can't stand still,
I haven't the will.

Straight ahead, the whisper said,
The one I heard inside my head.
Onward and forward will I tread,
By my Saviour I am led.

Sandra Voyce
Wales

LITTLE DONKEY

I paused beside a farmyard gate
To rest, one summer's day
And in the field, beneath a tree,
A little donkey lay.
He looked so peaceful lying there
The grass so fresh and green.
I closed my eyes and I could see
A very different scene.
The little donkey seemed the same,
Humble, grey and small,
But on his back a precious load,
A man, the friend of all.
The way was rough, the noonday sun
Was hot upon his head.
But sure and firm the donkey trod
The dusky road ahead.
The noise and bustle all around
As people flocked to see
The king, who soon would go to die
To save someone like me
How different is this tranquil scene
The pasture where you lie
The gentle breeze to cool the air
The river running by.
You bore the son of God that day
Your task so nobly done
So you have truly earned your rest
And shade from noonday sun.

K Woodford
Scotland

POEM FOR TURKEY

We've stood amongst the ancient stones and heard of times long past,
We've looked at cities ignoring God and have seen how they didn't last.
A culture bearing presents - tea at every turn
Lord, that they'd see you for real and thirst for the things of Heaven.
That the amphitheatres of old would resound with the gospel news
And Turkey once again dear Lord would repent and turn to you.
That lives would be restored, rebuilt, united in your name,
That the workers would be many and the harvest just the same.
That the windows of Heaven would open and pour out
Many abundant blessings to end all spiritual drought.

As we've seen the waterways which channelled ancient springs
And worshipped God amidst the ruins singing praises to our King.
May we remember Turkey and the people living there,
May we seek your face dear Lord in frequent constant prayer.
Let us be as living stones built for you to dwell within
Faithful to your calling, redeemed, set free from sin.
That each nation represented here would see your kingdom come.
Obedient to your word O God committed to your son.
Thank you for your mercy, thank you for your grace,
We know that you go with us as we travel from this place.
Guide each one in righteousness, let your will be done,
Keep us faithful unto you 'til Jesus Christ returns.

E Brady
Scotland

THE WAVES IN MY HEART

I place the shell against my ear
There I hear the sea.
I may be miles away from shore
But the waves have come to me.

It's just a little miracle,
That I don't understand,
Nature's precious music box
Ocean brought to land.

Of all the times I searched for you,
As I travelled paths of woe.
I wanted you to be there,
But how would I know?

I looked for signs in rainbows,
In the miracle of birth,
Flowers in the meadow,
Designs of heavenly worth.

My eyes damp with tears,
Still I could not see,
'Show me please, I want to know,
Are you there for me?'

I lift my head and then look through
The haze of swollen eyes,
I see the shell and understand
The mist begins to rise.

Signals and signs cannot be seen
Just like the waves I hear.
Now when I listen to my heart
Your love is loud and clear.

Lee Lanciotti
Wales

Untitled

As we travel on Life's journey,
With the future still unknown.
If we only trust in Jesus,
We shall never be alone.

So when trials and temptations,
Press us down on every side,
Just a little talk with Jesus,
Asking him to be our Guide.

When temptation overcomes us,
And we stumble on the way,
With his hands he gently leads us,
Back upon the narrow way.

He will help us through the trials,
That all Christians have to bear.
We can fight our battles bravely,
When we know our Lord is there.

He will teach us to be humble,
Thinking not of self alone.
Only anxious to help others,
Find the way to his dear Throne.

We can trust in him completely,
He will never let us down.
Till at last we go to Heaven,
To receive his promised Crown.

Gwen Pemberton
Wales

A NEW HEART
(A testimony)

'Twas in the early fifties
A preacher came to say,
'Listen men and brethren
Upon the Saviour's part,
He has made a promise,
To all people a new heart.'

I'd been in doubting castle,
I'd fought with giant despair,
But doubts and fears subsided,
When I cast on Him my care.

So now I've journeyed onward,
Travelled many paths in life,
I've trusted in the Lord daily,
Through joys or times of strife.

Now I'm looking forward,
To what He has in store,
For He has gone before me,
To open Heaven's door.

I know through three score years and ten,
The Saviour's borne my part,
Since in the early fifties,
He gave me a clean new heart.

G Walford Davies
Wales
(With His Lord in glory)

DEAR LORD

Dear Lord, please allow me a little time out
I am so tired, so weary and worn
This heart's been shattered, beaten and torn
I hurt all over, my confidence gone
Sorrow engulfs me, for Heaven I long.
I am so fragile, sensitive too
If only this, if only that
Many things in life I rue
Sometimes I see no light in this tunnel of mine
Often I'm lonely, rejected and cold
Now Lord I know, how it feels when you're old
For some, the journey through life is smooth and untossed
For others each day, trials and tests they unfold
One hurdle just over - another appears
Lost in a sea of confusion and tears
Oh help me to pray, my burdens to share
What would I do Lord, if you weren't there?
I get strength to survive from knowing you care.

'Sorrowmum'
Ireland

HAVING IT ALL

Get ready, we're told,
The millennium's coming.
A new year and new century.
Think of the opportunities!
Travel the world,
Get a new job,
Improve yourself
You can have it all!
Or instead,
We could stop and think
Of life and love
Of the sea whose tide we cannot control
Of the grass which grows by itself
And we could smile at our neighbour
And marvel at the God who has given us it all.

Alison Armstrong
Scotland

SUNSET

As I gaze out from my window
I sometimes close my eyes
To recall and to remember
All the beauty in the skies.

The sun is slowly sinking
Its colours changing fast
Clouds dressed in blue and turquoise
Turning pink are racing past.

The sun gives up its golden hue
As it settles below the clouds
Having brightened our lives for an hour or two
It is enveloped in the evening shrouds.

The wonders of God's great Heaven
Have passed before my eyes
And I am left with a tranquil afterglow
Until tomorrow's new sunrise.

A Haythorne
Scotland

My Impossible Dream

Lord, I love to feel wind, fresh wind in my hair,
To run in the sand, as if I was bare.
Watch a bright moon, shining on a cool sea,
Oh how dear Lord I wish this was me.

I love to watch the sea when it's calm,
And sit on a beach beneath a tall palm.
Delight in watching a star in the sky,
Learn more of your world, as each day goes by.

Lord teach us the way in which we should live,
By learning to love and wanting to give
To people around, who do not have much.
Poor people who really just live in a hutch.

I wish I could learn, what life's all about,
So I could stand up and give a great shout.
What a wonderful world, this really could be,
If we opened our eyes and we really could see.

Matilda Mitchell
Scotland

GIVE ME LOVE

Give me love
As a leaf dripping with dew
Give me love
Reaching out to help
With everyone who needs
Mend my cracks
And sew me up
Make me whole
And as I reach out
Comfort me
And make me new
I want to be transformed
I want to be just like you.

Heidi A Swanson
Scotland

GIVE THANKS

Give thanks for the sun up in the sky,
And the brightness as it shines,
Give thanks for the sky and clouds above,
And the moon and stars so fine.

Give thanks for the air around us,
It's so pure and fresh and free,
Give thanks for the mighty ocean,
And the rivers and the sea.

Give thanks for water pure and sweet,
Without this no one would know,
The happiness of life on earth,
Or the trees and flowers that grow.

Give thanks the Lord created us,
And every living thing,
Give thanks to him and him alone,
When we pray and when we sing.

Marjory Davidson
Scotland

A MUSE ON CREATION

Alone at last Lord you and me
upon the mountain under a tree -
such stillness is deafening.
Who could transpose the music of the wind upon the ear?
With bumbling bee and rabbit keen
there for a moment and then not seen.
Flies and midges zoom past
like racing cars going too fast.
The flowers they bob to and fro
dancing unrehearsed in full bloom they go.
Oh, the smell of the rose as it blends with the mayflower.
Crashing of waves, a trickle in the stream but the sea holds its power
liquid gold of the sun upon the silver sea.
Jesus you alone set us free.
Oh what fullness of senses, on what delight
great is our God and yet this is a fraction of his might!

R Hogg
Wales

IN HIS TIME

In my searching I have found
when seed is scattered on the ground,
the minute miracles seem to know
when the time has come to grow.
They need the sun, they need the rain
to grow too soon, they'd feel the pain
of cold, cold days that are not nice
and soon they'd feel they'd paid the price
of rushing up before the time,
that God had planned to be their prime.
As I rush here and there each day
I hear a voice that seems to say.
'Calm down Sue and be a seed.
Trust in me is all you need.
I have a plan for your whole life,
so why this rushing and this strife?'

W Lacey
Wales

GOD BE MERCIFUL TO ME A SINNER

We enter this world so small and helpless
Yet so young and innocent, we still transgress,
Time passes quickly, we remain unchanged.
We meander through life by others misled.

The Bible tells us we must confess
The sin from birth that we possess.
All have sinned, no one is exempt,
Except for Jesus, our Saviour heaven sent.

We can go to Church and sing aloud,
Read and pray and repeat the Creed,
How easy to look so pious to others
Elevating ourselves with many stories.

Humility, the gift that's required of us
So difficult to achieve, but precious,
We must bow down and seek God's power,
To possess it and aim to persevere.

Jesus said, the humble will be exalted.
Kneel in His presence and be justified,
We'll know His blessing and happiness,
As our faith from day to day increases.

I Campbell
Ireland

A PRAYER

Let me love you more each day,
And if I do not always feel
Your presence within my soul,
Let me not become despondent,
Rather, let me remember that
You have said: 'I am with you always.'
That is your priceless gift to me,
The pledge of your unconditional love,
And I believe in your word.
I believe that you are with me
In all the circumstances of my life,
That you watch over me,
That you know me better
Than I know myself.
Even when my heart grows cold
And I forget about you,
You do not forget about me.
You keep on loving me.
You do not give up on me.
You wait patiently,
And at the right moment
You melt my cold heart.
You take me by the hand
And lead me gently out of my darkness.
You hold me in your loving arms,
Close to your Good Shepherd heart,
And my love for you is rekindled.
You make my soul sing again.
You are my Father.

Maurice McAleese
Ireland

THE NEW MILLENNIUM

We like to get new things
New clothes, new books, new food,
So entering a new millennium
Is surely something good.

We should have new ambitions,
New ideas to help in need.
New plans for useful charities
New ways good work to lead.

New peace to settle conflicts,
New ways to work with others
New hope for closer contact
With strangers, friends, and brothers.

Let Christ into your life,
Let Him His grace impart,
He can make all things new
If dwelling in your heart.

The millennium then will give
A chance to serve Heaven's King
As in His steps we follow
And to Him praises bring.

Ella Smith
Ireland

THE FIRST DAY OF THE WEEK

Then cometh Mary, while darkness remained
Love that propelled her, could not be restrained
The disciples had left, gone to their home,
Mary stands rooted, as thoughts overcome.
While all around are lost in sleep
She is lost in sorrow and continues to weep
Down she stoops and looks into the sepulchre
Curious angels ask, 'What are you weeping for?'
'They have taken my Lord, I know not where!'
Then she turned, someone was standing there.
'Woman why weepest thou? Who do you seek?'
She answered, tears rolling down her cheek,
'Sir, if you have taken him, tell me where!'
She thinks, the gardener is standing there.
Then away goes her sorrow, despair and fear
His one word meant three, 'I am here.'
'Mary,' her name was all that he said.
Her master's voice, she is no longer misled.
She turned again, but turned not away
A rapturous, 'Rabboni,' was all she could say.
Then joy upon joy carried her feet along
The message he gave her, made her strong,
'Tell my brethren what I have told you.
I ascend to my Father and your Father too.'

Sarah Smeaton
Ireland

THE VOICE IN MY HEART

Mankind is in peril if it hears not my word
Said a voice, said a voice in my heart,
For I will come, I will come like a thief in the night
Said the voice, said the voice in my heart,
And all that men worship and all of his deeds
Will be slain by the sword of my truth,
I will take my beloved away from the earth
Said the voice, said the voice in my heart.

The day of my coming draws nearer for men
Said the voice, said the voice in my heart,
So prepare Ye the way, prepare Ye the way
Said the voice, said the voice in my heart,
And gather my children and say unto them
That the day of the Lord is at hand,
And if they won't listen, then cast them aside
Said the voice, said the voice in my heart.

I am the shepherd that gathers his flock
Said the voice, said the voice in my heart,
And I've known you and loved you for all of your days
Said the voice, said the voice in my heart,
For I am the way and the truth and the light
The light of all lights in the world,
So go into all nations and tell them . . . I come!
Said the voice, said the voice in my heart.

Mike Smith
Scotland

TEDDYCARE

He lolls upon the topmost stair,
You'd hardly notice he was there,
But for the fact that he exudes
A rather melancholy air.

Once happy in the nursery lair,
Who only craved a little care,
But handed down, he did become
A sorry, tattered, one-eyed bear.

Thus must he rest in mute despair,
With growl-box long beyond repair,
A tangled, mangled hopeless case,
A wreck, a wrack, a threadbare bear.

Yet see the child ascend the stair,
She'd thought him lost, oh such a scare!
Scoops gladly up her fraying friend,
Her lop-lugged, well hugged, cherished bear.

Should we condemn, would it be fair
To judge a child on tattered bear?
A tangled mess he well may be,
It matters not, if love is there.

Lorna Pearson
Wales

THE MIRACLE

(Based on Ecclesiastes 11 v 6: 'In the morning sow your seed, and at evening withhold not your hand; for you do not know which may prosper, this or that, or whether both will be alike good.')

I saw the little seed fall to the earth below;
It seemed too small to germinate, much less to grow.
Scarce able to believe it,
With naught to do but leave it,
In wond'ring impotence I turned to go.

One solitary seed exposed upon the ground
Where hostile forces, menacing, surround -
Those which would trample, beat it,
Drown it, exhaust or eat it:
Could it, perhaps, survive where such abound?

I went upon my way, full of my own life's care;
Forgot the tiny seed, forlornly lying there.
Much later, chancing by it,
I marvelled to espy it,
A blossom, glowing into the sunlit air.

Could this, in truth, be from that same small seed I'd sown,
Cast on the earth, defenceless and alone?
Then had my God detected it,
Had nourished and protected it,
Till suddenly mature and known.

Robert A Hardwidge
Scotland

THE CRUCIFIXION

Man's tragic sin became God's victory.
He fashioned those events to suit His will.
He bore the blackest thing in history
And lives and ever reigns among us still.

He used the fearful Cross on which he died
To let mere mortals share the mystery
Of death o'ercome by resurrectiontide,
And now His Kingdom evermore shall be.

Frances Reed
Scotland

BLACKBIRDS' EVENSONG

I stood at the gate in the falling night,
The sky was softly darkening
With the sun glowing pink on the tree bark.
I heard the blackbird sing his evensong:
Clear notes resounding from tree to tree,
Echoed and answered by blackbirds near
and far;
Cutting through the dusk,
The warbled notes
Flowed out into the evening air;
Like liquid honey, dashed with quicksilver -
Like melted snow,
dripping off the branches -
They bounced off hedge and soil,
And floated high away to a new dawn,
As our praise in the night
Heralds the return of the Son!

Heather M Simpson
Ireland

A CHRISTMAS STAR

Diamond stars in velvet sky
Remind of time long gone,
When one great star's unfailing light
Above a stable shone.
A baby in a manger lay,
So gentle and so sweet,
And wise men seeking Royal birth
All worshipped at His feet.
The oxen and the little lamb
Lay down beside His bed,
And shepherds watching in the fields
All by that star were led.
And when we look into the night
And pray for peace on Earth,
The twinkling stars remind us of
That precious virgin birth.

Angela George
Wales

NEXT TIME ROUND

A ring of truth that peeled the world around
And returned a million echoes on a whispering veil of sound
But the Song of Songs it fades and withers on the wind
And what have we done and how have we sinned.

So where to now in these sad and darker days
When everyone wins and everything pays

He was still a man, however widely read
He was still a man and still he's dead

Next time he's back with a management team
Fighting fit, laconic, lean
Backed by the power of US cable
Guild the lily, build the fable
But will they believe what they cannot see
It's a question of faith and sanity.

Douglas Lawrie
Scotland

THE TEN COMMANDMENTS

All people who on earth do dwell
Should the Ten Commandments heed
Let me tell you they are swell
If practised in everyday life, indeed.

What could be more true - without pain
No other gods we shall go craving
Nor shall we take the Lord's name in vain
No swearing, no open shops for Sunday trading.

Your parents you should heed
You should not kill or maim your fellow man
Another man's wife you should not need
Nor pilfer from your neighbour's van.

If everyone these commandments did uphold
A much better place this earth would seem
No wars, no fighting, no Aids we are told
And even death would not seem so mean.

Beth McCracken
Ireland

A . . .

I am a rolling stone,
That is no more,
Still and silent cold to the touch,
What was has gone,
Embedded in the dust.

I have rolled to a place,
So low it is bare,
Just empty souls are scattered here.
But can I drag myself out,
Or will I live a life of despair?

I need strength,
But I need help to get there.
I need to believe,
But who is there?

A prayer perhaps to relieve the pain,
A church to go to, to help get through the mundane.
A choice of life something to believe,
A once lost soul breathes deep.

Clare Ann Horridge
Wales

LAST WORDS

Father forgive them what they do.
Those who condemned Me.
Those who flogged Me.
The soldiers who mocked Me,
crowned My head with thorns,
then nailed My hands and feet to a cross.

Bless those who wept for Me,
on that sorrowful journey to Calvary.
Simon, who helped carry My cross,
Veronica, who wiped My face,
the gypsy boy who hid one of the nails
meant for my feet.

Console My Blessed Mother,
at the foot of My cross weeping.
Father please accept My Spirit into Thy keeping.

Doris Rowe
Scotland

CELEBRATING THE MILLENNIUM

I never thought I'd see the millennium
And celebrate the birth of Him
Two thousand years ago.

But now it looks like it's going to be.
I am old, but fit, and can still see,
And only four months to go.

How will I celebrate my Jesus' birth?
Not with parties, fireworks and mirth,
Loud voices and drinks that flow.

At the year two thousand I'll be at home,
And nowhere near the new-built dome.
I shall be praising Him alone.

A Kellie
Scotland

NODDFA CHAPEL, SUNDAY NIGHTLY

(Until destroyed by fire, Noddfa chapel - the cathedral of the Rhondda - was a massive edifice to valley non-conformity)

To Noddfa, chapel, Sunday nightly
Parading Rhondda Christians go.
To Hermon, Carmel the meek and mighty
Come from terrace and miners' row.

In Noddfa chapel, Sunday nightly
Hands scoured clean, and Sunday best
Is mummified in mothballed piety,
And weekday sins are all confessed.

Through Noddfa chapel Sunday nightly
Lofty, then their anthems ring -
Surging solfa psalms and anthems
As the four-part chorus sings.

From Noddfa chapel, Sunday nightly
Rhondda Christians home recoil
Fortified by prayers and sermons
To face another week of toil.

No more to Noddfa, Sunday nightly
Nor to Zion or Jerusalem
Pace expectant Rhondda pilgrims;
For the chapels have heard their last Amens.

John Jenkins
Wales

A PERFECT CHILD

God gave us a little child
Perfect in every way.
You gave us so much happiness
Before he called you away.

You used to run around all day
With your sisters and brothers, you would play.
Your loving face was a joy to all
I sometimes ask God, why he made that call.

We watched you suffer little one
But we knew you were waiting, for Jesus to come.
We sat by your bed and held your hand
This was something we never planned.

Then Jesus came, placed his hand on your head
You turned and smiled, enough was said.
He gently closed your tired eyes
Sleep in peace our perfect child.

F Davies
Wales

UNTITLED

God in His almighty hands
Holds all Creation in their bands,
And by decree His works fulfil
Holds heaven and earth within His will.

Spans the millennia, wise, unseen
Constant in the changing scenes,
The Law and Order strong and stout
In a fickle world of doubt.

Before His throne all things obey
All things according to their way,
His Word is Law, who can ignore
His bounteous nature without flaw.

Commands the seas, the raging storm
And in His clasp are lightnings born,
From these things we stand in awe
Thanks to Him, His mercies all.

Thro' Satan's lie came death
For which is now condemned,
But to the world came Christ
Now darkened ways enlightened.

And thro' His Saviour Son
Repentance bringeth pardon,
Our yoke is lightened such
That sin has no dominion.

For now we all rejoice
Thro' love and grace abounding,
And all with faithful voice
Sing praises for God's favours.

K C Thomas
Wales

PERSONS, PUZZLES AND PRAISE

A Trinity of persons doth
Provoke some minds to think, 'Enough!
This dogma is too high for me
If three is one and one is three.'
Such riddle-seekers fail to see
That fellowship is just the key
To solving of this mystery
Where three is one and one is three.

A Trinity of persons might
Encourage some to think, 'All right!
Perhaps it means God's not alone
If one is three and three is one.'
For once the mathematics' done,
Were God alone there could be none
For us to call 'Father' and 'Son'.
But one is three and three is one.

A Trinity of persons ought
To make us think, 'I have been taught!
My mouth with praises will resound
As in God one and three are found.
Now in my life there is a ground
For fellowship with those around.
Community will now abound
Since in God three and one are found.'

A Baird
Ireland

THE WORLD

'I believe' we have a maker
Architect and great creator.
Gift of thought has been ordained
Sadly used and badly stained,
Creating what it thought was order
Reaching often saneless border.
Talently they play with toy
Mad inventions to destroy
Spaces that could fruit neglected
Places to destroy invented
Then they say, we are too many
Weeding out, a costly penny
Lean and hungry always pleading
Sustenance is all they're needing
Challenging the will of reason
Seeking pill for active season
Gift of *Atom* for the nation
For their help and not pollution
Great thinking, lost their way
For stupid folly they will pay,
Turn back I say, from roaring torrent
Avoid the horrors, so abhorrent
This I'm sorry cannot be
While the intellect is free
It is not true what people say
That science made the night and day
With their thought and eyes all seeing
Accept the guidance of supreme being
Using gift for human need
Simply guided by the creed . . .

F N F
Wales

GOD ON YOUR SIDE

God is waiting on your call
and His line is free to-day.
He knows you're in deep trouble,
you have some things to say.

I have already told Him
you don't know what to do,
but God insists it's personal
He'd rather talk to you.

Sure He knows all your problems
He's dealt with them before.
Somehow this time is different
Just let Him know the score.

He knows the great uncertainties
of commitments you have made.
He wants to reassure you
and tell you not to be afraid.

The line is still kept free for you -
your questions to unfold,
God's got all the answers
written in His book of gold.

The air time you're allotted
for your heavenly interview
was specially requested
by friends who are loving you.

Mary J Devlin
Ireland

I Need You

You went and died at Calvary,
Standing in the place of me.
Your blood it flowed
To cleanse and set us free
Who answered to your call
And cried, 'Forgive Me!'
I need you.

I praise you for my life on earth.
For giving me my second birth.
I give to you my life, my all,
For I am nothing, no I'm nothing without you.
I need you.

May I hear your voice so sweet,
May my spirit with you meet.
As friend to friend may we speak
Your fellowship I'll always seek.
Stay by me, inside me.
I need you.

You are my strength,
You are my power.
The very breath I take each hour.
Of every minute, second of each day
Oh Lord hear me as I pray and touch me.
I need you.

I McDonald
Scotland

YOUR SPECIAL FRIEND

If you're feeling down,
Then don't frown,
Just look up at the sky,
There will be no need to cry,
Cause there is your special friend.

You'll always have other friends good or bad,
The one thing is he will never get mad,
So just lift up your tears,
And throw away your fears,
For he will always be with you.

Friends will come and go,
But he will always know,
When you are feeling down,
He'll place upon your head a crown,
And will never leave you no matter what.

Leeanne Harrison
Scotland

ISAIAH 12

Jehovah's wrath had threatened me
For from my God I'd turned my face.
I begged forgiveness, and received.
Praise the Almighty for His grace.

Now God with me, my fear is gone.
All trust in Him who rescued me.
My heart with joyous music swells:
His strength is my serenity.

For I was thirsty, desperate,
Till at life's spring I had my fill.
And Oh what Joy! My thirst is quenched;
The saving Fount unquenchable.

And so my lips must praise and thank
My great Redeemer for His word.
The story of His 'whelming love . . .
Oh wondrous day when all have heard!

Yes, let the whole wide world rejoice
In Him whose love our spirit thrills.
Let all creation praise His worth,
And marvel at His miracles.

You citizens of Zion's hill
Extol the Lord with utter zest.
Almighty God dwells in your midst;
What ecstasy to be thus blessed!

George Newall
Scotland

HEAVEN'S WELCOME

Those with eyes that cannot see
Those with ears that cannot hear
Or with legs that cannot walk
They all belong to Thee!

In a land beyond our sight
The blind will one day see
The deaf will hear you calling
'Oh come dear ones to me!'

Then shall eyes behold Thee
Ears will hear Thy voice
Legs will run towards Thee
And Heaven will rejoice!

Marguerite Brassington-Griffiths
Wales

THE PARABLE OF THE UNFORGIVING DEBTOR
(Matthew 18: 23-35)

I'll tell you a story
You'll never forget;
It's a tale full of worry -
A man was in debt.
He owed his employer
Some five thousand pounds;
The interest went higher
And leapt up in bounds.

He wept and he wailed
And he begged on his knees;
His master forgave him
Because he said, 'Please.'
Relief of the tension,
The gladness, the joy,
And no one would mention
He'd been a bad boy.

He met on the way home
The bloke from next door,
Of shabby appearance,
All ragged and poor:
'I gave you a fiver
Last week for some bread -
Now pay up you waster,
Or else you'll be dead!'

But now the employer
He heard of the tale;
And the five thousand debtor
Was trembling and pale.
Forgive your transgressor
And try to forget,
For old human nature
Is always in debt.

James Henry Jones
Wales

ARE BY FAR

We are but mere accessors to, Thy golden shrine so shrill
To each a life, that was well spent, in humble dwelling still.
Where e'er the reason why is clear, we do, so mercilessly say
Dear God, you are of wondrous awe, this night we lowly pray.
You reach, a dream in night, unto the morning star.
Across the wide expanse of space, you truly are by far,
The most important part of man, that he could ever own
And the deeds that he would share, for none he did atone.
Did not atone, did not say sorry, not even unto death,
That man did cause, your son oh Lord, the pain of Calvary
But you were more, than human Lord, and rose above death's kneel
On the day of three, you did rise again, beyond pain, had no feel
And there it's with us, unto now, we're here within God's plan,
That our faults and sins, are atoned thereof, and accredited unto man.
For what we have, we hold as one, the task through life, that's just
begun.

God we measure and decree, when that which said, we call to thee,
But then again, to greater task, that heralds belief, just why they ask.
I have before me, life extreme, the crooked corner, the empty chair,
Too good, too bad, too often soon, that I am here and oft aware.

Beyond me there is one such aim, that does shine forth, of one acclaim,
By then a purpose, there reigns the call
For that's God's standard for us all.
We do have of our angels, to guide us, there along
To ferry us, where ere we go, be safe, by night and day,
And we are of, just one thereto, for all of ages pray.

Hugh Campbell
Ireland

THE THIN RED LINE

The thin red line went back and forth
across the country road
unaware of the danger yet to come
no one could tell them
or make them change their way
as they moved along the line of their food chain run
the tiny red ants were on the move
on this quiet country road
but through the ant hill
a drain was marked
as the white line clearly showed
if only I could warn them
said a traveller along the way
but I would have to become an ant
for them to understand
what I have to say
our lives are like the little red ant
as we cross this road called life
God looks down on us
and sees, our grief and strife
he sent His son amongst us
to help us on our way
to show us the danger on the road,
and where not to stray.

Frank Scott
Ireland

PAX VOBISCUM!

Today a scrieve in joyful vein
for me, life's fu o fun'
do tell me Muse what's next tae scrieve
an whit remains tae come.
That letter that a got this morn -
'for yeir support, my thanks'
gies hope for me tae ken ma freen
will sune rejoin oor ranks
an aince again wi courteous voice
cause havoc wi ma views
by questionin ma verra faith -
ma future life's 'good news'
frae the standpoint o a man
wha has endured the final test
an nou embarks on life, alane,
his wife, in peace, at rest!
The fun in life, at times far gone
remains whether seen or not
and the hand that took can gie again
ere we too, face the spot.
Hae courage, freen, tae face the way
alang yeir lanely road
an may it end in peace an quiet
in the presence o yeir Goad!

Andrew A Duncan
Scotland

BEWARE OF CORNERS

Lurking in the corners
Keeping out of sight,
Nasty little devils
Full of evil might.

Evil thoughts are hidden,
Evil words less so,
Evil deeds will flourish
If we let them grow.

Churchmen knew the answer
How their souls to save;
When they built their churches
Built a rounded nave.

D Richardson
Scotland

WALKING THE ROAD

Two men who were walking along the road
Came to a halt when they saw a crowd
Being inquisitive - they stopped - to see
What was the cause of this melee.
Did someone faint? What were they doing?
What were this large crowd viewing?

There was a man - amidst the crowd
Standing talking to those around.
Someone queried - 'Who is this?'
'Oh, just a man who said that he
Could heal the blind - and make them see.'

Who was this man? By now, you will know
They are stories of a long time ago.
He gave his life for you and me
By dying there on Calvary.

Jean Logan
Scotland

MEANT TO BE

You were meant to be
It was no accident
Yesterday I turned back the pages
In my book of memories
To where I was when I met you -
In the church, an old visitor book
Where, we found our names together!
It was God's providence to meet
We lit a lot of candles!
Will our names be found again?
In God's book of life.

Irene Grant
Scotland

WHAT'S IN A NAME

The Millennium is nearly here two thousand years have past
Since Jesus Christ was born for us, a King of Peace at last.
He didn't come in robes of silk or crown upon his head,
But as a babe born in a barn, a manger for his bed.

When he grew to be a man, he toured the countryside
Preaching to the people who listened what he said.
And by the sea of Galilee he cured the sick and lame
He even made the blind to see this added to his fame.

People said the lame and sick were cured by their own faith
If that is so, maybe this world would be a better place.
The faith that men had long ago was instilled in us today
And men would live in peace and love and follow in his way.

No wars, no troubles by greedy men, like those so long ago
Who killed the Lord upon the cross, to please their own ego.
But Jesus didn't die in vain, he died that we might live
And all our wrongs and all our sins, did lovingly forgive.

Famous men have come and gone, their names are lost in time
We live and die our names forgot, even yours and mine.
But after two thousand years, one name lives on today
The name of Jesus Christ our Lord, that is a name to stay.

M Purdon
Scotland

HIS WORLD

Why did God make people?
To walk across pebbles,
To destroy earth
To destroy it,
Why?

Why do we destroy
For fun?
No.
For pleasure?
No.
Why don't we recycle everything?
Why do some people drop bombs?
To destroy people, animals,
And the environment.
Why do we use CFC's and kill,
To make us look nice.
To destroy,
Why?

I could ask these questions several times
Why? Why? Why?
Why did God make people
To destroy *His World.*

Eleri Phylip Davies
Wales

A Smile Goes Further Than A Sigh

Even though the outward man perishes,
yet the inward man is being renewed day by day
2 Cor 4:16

Though courage fails, hope cleaves the rock
A brave smile goes further than a sigh,
And if you choose to seek the good things
You'll find that they will multiply.

Daily blessings are daily reminders of One
Who soothes the heart that's grieved, and pained
So many times when hope was flagging
He has rescued and sustained.

The secret in life is not what one likes
But to like what one has to do.
And the heart that keeps its faith alight
Raises the spirits of others too.

To carry small stones will eventually move
The mountain that you now face,
No need to dread what lies ahead
When upheld by excelling grace.

Doreen Craig
Ireland

I CANNOT GO BACK

My life has gone forward, I cannot go back.
I've taken a few faltering steps up life's long track.

Days seemed long and hard, the pace seemed so slow.
But God kept my hand in his. 'Child, onward we'll go.'

'The past is behind us now; keep holding my hand,
On through life's troubles together we'll stand.'

But dark clouds did gather, afraid and alone,
I thought I was abandoned and couldn't go on.

But He'd gently remind me of his loving care.
'You're never alone My Child, I'll always be there.'

He reminds me each day now of his loving touch.
The way he has prepared for me; he loves me that much.

'I'll walk with you daily, right by your side.
I'll show you rich treasures and much more beside.'

Lord, I want to walk with you, on life's busy way.
Wherever you lead me, Lord, help me to stay.

Stay loving and faithful, right to the end.
My Precious Redeemer, My Saviour and Friend.

So as I now follow down life's long path;
You've made me and changed me, I cannot go back.

Carol A Laing
Scotland

INCHMAHOME PRIORY

Rising from Holy mist,
Your whalebacked shadow
Pits light against shade,
Allows sunscapes, wetwinds,
To move as one across
Your ringwort face.

The Lake of Menteith
Could never comprehend
Those hardedged sobrieties
That turned flesh into spirit;
Your explosion of joy
Behind the guiding light.

History began here
With a canticle sung
By raw-boned acolytes,
It ended in a grey
Haired orison that froze
A tonsured dream.

Your yesterday's parables,
Those happy vigils,
Sleep safe under a
Straddle Moon, while
Your Gospel, thrives beyond
A pagan haunted shore.

James Adams
Scotland

THE SPIDER'S MASTERPIECE . . . JAN 22ND (1999)

The garden was drenched with fog today,
As I gazed from my windowpane,
What could that be on the clothes line?
'Twas not there yesterday.

I eagerly went out and saw
A vision of lace and filigree,
Heart shaped, and wondrous to behold,
In perfect symmetry.

The frost had made it crisp and white,
A beautiful sight to see.
I scarcely could believe my eyes,
Oh God! You are good to me.

I was the only one to see it there;
On that morn so cold and chill.
Within an hour it had vanished,
But it shines in my memory still.

Marjorie Jones
Wales

CHANGE

When I look for the evidence
It's there
Though it's opposite to common sense,
Somewhere
In my life something changed

How can I be so certain?
I don't know
But there will be no final curtain
In this show

Death to life - something changed

Can I show you what it is?
I'm unable
Is it certainty that lives?
Or a fable

Deep in my heart something changed

Could it happen to anyone?
Yes it can
Just believe, you don't have to
Understand

This is love, let Him in, let Him change you.

B Pettiford
Wales

MILLENNIUM

Christ came to earth two millenniums ago
The love of God the Father to show
Born of a Virgin, miraculous birth
No other like it in all the earth
While here He lived a sinless life
Midst all the turmoil, trouble and strife
Showing compassion, giving sweet rest
To the weary and laden with sin oppressed
How great His compassion, how true His love
What matchless grace come down from above
As the end of the second millennium draws nigh
We're assured of His coming again in the sky
The signs of the times show it could be quite soon
Be prepared to meet Him, for unprepared could mean doom.

R B Mckenzie
Ireland

A CLOUDED DARKNESS

When we are born on Heaven's door
a light of light from the dimness
heart a temple of life
eyes are opening
a fortress built around us
life beginning for the new dawn.

The morning sun
breath sheds no fear
silver streams running
oceans beyond horizons
a clouded darkness
We must lift our souls
Heaven's calling
not beyond our life.

Our lives united by a world that's changed
ashes rising shading the moon!
into darkness
God deep in our minds
bodies open from mother's blood.
Weeping willows woodland wilt and fade.

Our last stand let us rise
naked eyes look up to a stone-washed sky
God be with us
don't fear the bed of evil
the temple turning to dust
as we rise into the holy night
peace.

Garrett John
Wales

THANK YOU GOD AT HARVEST TIME

We'd like to thank you once again,
For giving us our food -
The fruit, the corn, the wheat, the bread
And vegetables that are good.

We'd like to thank you for the sun,
The wind, and rain too.
The trees, the flowers, the grass so green.
Oh Lord, we thank you.

June Legg
Wales

THE PLAN

Behind all the tinsel
glitter and glow,
Stands Jesus of Nazareth
the babe who did grow
into the Saviour
of the world.
Ignoring the insults
and the way they were hurled.

Thank God this child
became a man.
Lived-breathed-endured
Then died for us
He was the plan.

Shirley Wharton
Scotland

NEW YEAR PRAYER

A year, untouched, lies just ahead - a precious gift from God
A gateway to a fresh approach, to serve our mighty Lord
Please grant us peace, and joy, and love within this
bright New Year,
Protect us from all evil, and bless what we hold dear,
Dear Father if it be your will, then give us eyes
to see,
The truth that lies within your word, and let it
set us free,
Lord give us strength to tread your paths, and
guide your steps to you,
That all may see the Saviour's love, in everything
we do.
The very best that we could do, would never be
enough,
So help us to obey your word, in Jesus we will
trust,
Let resolution be for us to worship constantly,
and by your grace gain knowledge, of very high
degree.
The year two thousand beckons like a bright and
shining star,
God grant this brand next century, a final end
to war.

Amen

A Hausrath
Scotland

EMANUEL

God with us - Emanuel
Come as a babe that all may see His humanity.
Not as a king o'er man to reign in sovereignty.
But lowly lies, within a stable bare, the Christ-child
'Jesus' - as the Angel did declare.
Born of a virgin that mankind might know
Freedom from sin and life abundant here below.

God with us - Emanuel
Come worship with me now, bow down in deep humility.
For in such presence who can fail to bow the knee.
God come in person, just to rescue and deliver those
Born in sin, that they may live for ever.
Spend now they days in praise of His salvation
Until He gathers out His own - from every nation.

God with us - Emanuel.
Why has it happened thus? Why did God so appear?
Was it that man no longer needs to fear, no longer
Needs to dwell in bondage or in doubt.
God has provided in His Son - His own way out
View not alone a babe among the hay, but
Think again the debt Christ had to pay, and -
Stand again beneath a centre cross at Calvary
Pausing to realise - God sent His Son for me!

God with us - Emanuel
What joy - what hope rises within the trusting soul.

Christ, risen indeed, made by His Spirit whole
And all because 2,000 years ago - God sent His Son
In such a simple way, to gladden hearts that first
                  glad Christmas Day.
Now we await, as promised in God's word
A second coming of God's Son - our Lord.
Noel. Noel - New birth - Emanuel.

S McCloskey
Ireland

THE DECISION

My heart was heavy
And full of despair.
The way was dark
No light was there.
So, I sorted out my thinking
I knew just what to do
I'll parcel up those troubles, Lord
And leave them all with you.
Your law of adjustment begins, and then
Harmonious living once more will reign.
The peace of your presence
Is by my side
My thoughts are at peace
Now my heart is light.

Nan Ogg
Scotland

NIGHT

As the shades of night are falling the golden sun sinks
in the west and the silver moon comes to shine as she
glides through the sky the big clouds pass her by, she
sends her moonbeams to the ground casting shadows all
around, the owl hoots as he looks for his prey at the end
of the day. The nightingale sings his lullaby at twilight
as the sun sinks everything sleeps the gentle rain falls
pitter, patter, on my windowpane among the hedgerow and in
the long grass where the hedgehog sleeps disturbing not his
slumber, hidden, and unseen, the snail as slow as he can be
curls up against the wall the long grass hides him from our
view and you wouldn't know he was there at all, and the
spider's web glitters like a jewel it glittered and gleamed and
faded away. Then all at once there is a rainbow to be seen
high up above with colours red, and yellow, orange and green,
and in a moment it has faded away leaving the moon and the
stars to shine at the end of a perfect day.

Helen Manson
Scotland

A SPECIAL FRIEND

You're special to me;
When you smile
I see Jesus more clearly.
When you touch my hand,
I feel His presence
So much nearer.
I'm so grateful for your love;
Your patience and kindness
Teaches me more clearly
Of my God,
And when you go away,
It seems as though
The light has dimmed,
And my way is that much
More difficult to find.
God has taught me so much
Through you;
I will never stop thanking Him
For His grace and love
In giving you to me.
You're special to me,
My friend.

Patricia Davies
Wales

I UNDERSTAND

I understand critics who criticise each other,
And the correspondent's story differs from his colleagues.
And the solicitor, aware of his client's guilt,
Defends the criminal. Those are the faults of man.

I understand teachers who enthuse over the gifted,
Not so, to those without worldly talents;
Politicians who put party before people,
Scientists who exploit abominable discoveries.
Their ambitions get out of hand.

I understand Clergy who pat the backs of the military,
Hang war-torn flags alongside
Crucifixes of everlasting love and peace,
They mix patriotism with Christ's love of all people.

Christ has taught me the inconsistencies of the world.

It's not just evil people who are killed in conflict,
Where the good return home to their families.
Tradesman slay tradesman, murderer kills murderer,
Christian crucifies Christian, and the bomb devours all.
If the Devil could be seen, he could be slain.
Good people shield him unknowingly
Sacrificing their own kind,
Only to find Satan gone and their brothers'
Corpses lying at my feet.

Through the world of man, Christ's constant hand
Has led me through life's maze.
My life-long host, the Holy Ghost
Has taught me God's true ways.

Ken James
Wales